STUDYING FOOD WEBS

DESERT DINNERS

Studying Food Webs in the Desert

JULIE K. LUNDGREN

Rourke

Publishing LLC
Vero Beach, Florida 32964

www.rourkepublishing.com

Project Assistance:
The author thanks Yajaira Gray from the Center for Sonoran Desert Studies at the Arizona-Sonora Desert Museum, Tracy Nelson Maurer, and the team at Blue Door Publishing.

Photo credits:
Cover Photos: Eagle © HTuller, Snake © Casey K. Bishop, Rabbit © IRC, Flower © Lee & Marleigh Freyenhagen; Page 4 © Chris Curtis; Page 5 © Galyna Andrushko, Chris Curtis, Petrov Andrey, Casey K. Bishop, Page 6 © NASA Earth Observatory; Page 8 © Flominator, Infrogmation, ToB, vera bogaerts; Page 9 © Jarno Gonzalez Zarraonandia; Page 10 © douglas knight, PSHAW-PHOTO, Y6y6y6; Page 11 © MWaits, US NPS; Page 12 © Petrov Andrey; Page 13 © RTimages, John Hill, Vrlpep; Page 14 © HTuller; Page 15 © Martyman, KeresH (wiki), Berichard; Page 17 © Eric Lawton, HTuller, urosr, Snowleopard1, Vrlpep, Buquet, TZajaczkowski, Rex, IRC, Brian Weed, MWaits, PSHAW-PHOTO, Steffen Foerster Photography, Galyna Andrushko, Bertrand Collet, Sebastian Kaulitzki; Page 18 © Rex; Page 19 © PhotoSky 4t com, Page 19b © Dr. Heinz Linke; Page 20 © Paul Cowan; Page 21 © nialat; Page 22 © Peter Leahy; Page 23 © catnap, Lou Oates; Page 24 © Stephen Finn; Page 25 © MPF; Page 26 © erikdegraaf fotografie; Page 27 © Nick Carver Photography; Page 28 © Oleksandr Koval; Page 29 © photoBeard

Editor: Jeanne Sturm

Cover and page design by Nicola Stratford, Blue Door Publishing

Library of Congress Cataloging-in-Publication Data

Lundgren, Julie K.
  Desert dinners : studying food webs in the desert / Julie K. Lundgren.
    p. cm. -- (Studying food webs)
  ISBN 978-1-60472-315-1 (hardcover)
  ISBN 978-1-60472-780-7 (softcover)
  1. Desert ecology--Juvenile literature. 2. Food chains (Ecology)--Juvenile literature. 3. Deserts--Juvenile literature. I. Title.
  QH541.5.D4L86 2009
  577.54'16--dc22

Printed in the USA

CG/CG

Rourke Publishing
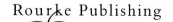
www.rourkepublishing.com – rourke@rourkepublishing.com
Post Office Box 3328, Vero Beach, FL 32964

Table Of Contents

On The Cover

Golden eagles in deserts prey on rabbits and snakes.

Venomous rattlesnakes eat small animals.

Jackrabbits nibble on grasses, seeds, and desert fruits.

Cacti provide food for desert herbivores.

Harnessing the Sun

All living things need sun, water, air, and food. A **food chain** links living things, each eaten by the one that follows it. Food chains begin with sunlight shining on green plants. Through **photosynthesis**, green plants transform the Sun's energy into food for living and growing. This food energy passes on to animals when the plants are eaten, and again when the animals are eaten. Because each living thing plays a role in many food chains, scientists call all of the food chains in an area a **food web**. The animals and plants in a food web depend on each other for survival.

During the brief days of moisture after a rare rainfall, North America's Sonoran Desert explodes with flowers. Desert plants jump into action when water is available.

CHEW ON THIS

Chlorophyll spurs the chemical reaction transforming light energy into food during photosynthesis. It colors the plants green, too.

This diagram shows the flow of a simple food chain, beginning with the Sun's energy and ending with an animal.

Weaving a Desert Web

A community of plants and animals and the ways they interact with each other and their surroundings form an **ecosystem**. Desert ecosystems cover a third of Earth's land. Hot or cold, hilly or flat, sandy or rocky, they all have one thing in common: deserts receive 10 inches (25 centimeters) or less of rain each year. Plants and animals must have **adaptations** to make their home in this parched habitat. They must have special ways to survive.

Although South America's Atacama, a cold winter desert, sits next to the Pacific Ocean, it receives the least amount of moisture of any place on Earth.

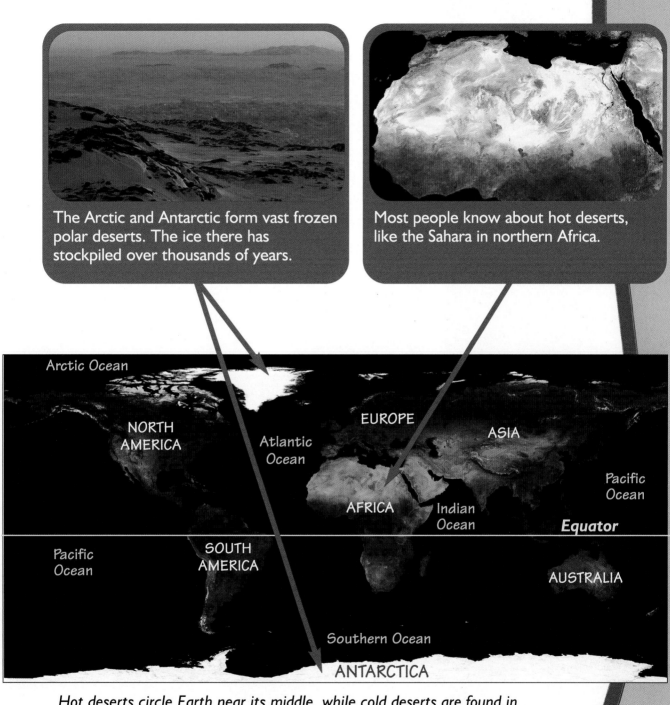

The Arctic and Antarctic form vast frozen polar deserts. The ice there has stockpiled over thousands of years.

Most people know about hot deserts, like the Sahara in northern Africa.

Arctic Ocean

NORTH AMERICA

Atlantic Ocean

EUROPE

ASIA

Pacific Ocean

AFRICA

Indian Ocean

Equator

Pacific Ocean

SOUTH AMERICA

AUSTRALIA

Southern Ocean

ANTARCTICA

Hot deserts circle Earth near its middle, while cold deserts are found in regions away from the equator.

Floating, microscopic organisms like diatoms and protozoa support throngs of tiny krill.

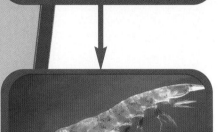

Krill support many animals, like Adelie penguins.

Adelie penguins guard their chicks and eggs from Antarctic skuas, another kind of bird.

Sizzling days and *brrr* cold nights challenge the plants and animals in hot deserts. Daytime temperatures climb to 120° Fahrenheit (49° Celsius) and plunge to near freezing after sunset. The dry, cloudless air allows the day's heat to escape out into space.

Cold deserts can be cold winter deserts or polar deserts. The polar deserts, found in the Arctic and Antarctic, are deserts of ice and extreme cold. Harsh conditions limit life here. Cold winter deserts support simple food chains of plants and animals that can withstand the seasonal changes in temperature.

Like a fanciful dream, a desert oasis springs up around a water source, supporting its own unique ecosystem.

CHEW ON THIS

El Azizia in Libya holds the record for the hottest temperature on Earth: 136° Fahrenheit (58° Celsius). Death Valley in California's Mojave Desert finishes second with a high of 134° Fahrenheit (57° Celsius).

What's for Dinner? Desert Dining

Transformers!

Plants, the **primary producers**, power up the desert ecosystem. The ability to store lots of water makes **succulents** like cacti, yuccas, and agaves suited to dry climates. Succulents have a waxy coating to keep them from drying out. Their barbed or sharp leaves protect against hungry (and thirsty) critters. Shrubs and grasses grow here, too. Desert plants have deep or wide root systems, or their seeds may simply wait for rain before sprouting.

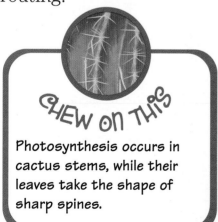

CHEW ON THIS

Photosynthesis occurs in cactus stems, while their leaves take the shape of sharp spines.

Yucca leaves resemble a bouquet of slicing swords.

This lone creosote bush's roots suck up all available water, leaving nothing for other plants attempting to grow near it.

The sharp barbs of agave leaves deflect plant eaters.

The Sonoran Desert's giant saguaro cacti attract insects, birds, and bats with their juicy branches, sweet fruit, and flower nectar.

Hunters and Gatherers

Herbivores, the **primary consumers**, nibble seeds, cacti, fruits, flower nectar, roots, green leaves, and grasses. Jerboas, kangaroo rats, and other rodents hide in their burrows by day and feed under the cool protective darkness of night. Jackrabbits, grasshoppers, ants, large herbivores, and others get most of the water they need from the plants they eat.

This nocturnal jerboa hops like a kangaroo. Its long back feet help it dig for roots, make a burrow, and pour on the speed when a hungry fox pursues it. Why do so many desert animals hop? Hopping uses less energy than walking or running.

CHEW ON THIS

Fruit eaters do plants a favor by spreading the plant's seeds in their scat, or waste.

The addax, a rare African antelope, can go months between drinks of water.

Carnivores hunt other animals. Those who eat primary consumers are **secondary consumers**. Common secondary consumers include many creepy crawlies, roadrunners, and bats. The giant desert centipede devours any animal it can overpower. It grows up to 8 inches (20 centimeters) long. Scorpions sting insects and millipedes with their venomous tails. Tarantulas prey on rodents, lizards, and small snakes. Shy rattlesnakes favor rodents. **Omnivores** like coyotes and foxes take advantage of the whole buffet: animals, plants, fruits, eggs, and insects. It's all game.

This giant desert centipede's body colors make it hard for another predator to decide which end is the head and which is the tail, allowing it a chance to escape.

Fennecs, found in North Africa and the Middle East, snap up anything the desert is serving that day: beetles, small lizards, rodents, roots, and eggs.

The desert ecosystem supports a few top predators. Eagles, hawks, and owls patrol the skies, while snow leopards, wolves, or bobcats prowl the land. These food chain kings must search wide areas to find enough food to survive.

Golden eagles can be found in the deserts, mountains, and grasslands of North America, Asia, and North Africa, using their keen eyesight to zero in on prey.

Eye On Australia

Amazing animals survive in Australia's wild interior. Red kangaroos are built to hop with long back feet and strong legs. By working together, clever dingoes occasionally nab these "big reds". Patient thorny devil lizards flick ants up one by one with their sticky tongues. Monitor lizards manage to swallow thorny devils despite their protective spikes. People have brought other animals here. Wild housecats, camels, and rabbits compete with **native** wildlife for available resources, and sometimes become dinner themselves.

Desert region

A thorny devil lizard shows its spikes to predators.

The perentie monitor lizard, also called the parenty, grows up to 8 feet (2.4 meters) long and weighs up to 33 pounds (15 kilograms). These skillful carnivores sprint after lizards, snakes, birds, rabbits, and large insects on their hind legs.

Moving On Up

Food webs describe the energy transfer from one living thing to another. Animals and plants are forms of stored energy. With each step in the food chain, energy is passed on and reduced. Plants use the Sun's energy to grow stems, leaves, and roots and to generate food. Now an herbivore eats the plants. It uses some of the energy to grow, but also uses some of the energy for daily living. When the herbivore is eaten, again it doesn't pass on all of the energy it ate, only what was stored.

In a food web, a large foundation of producers supports the consumers with energy from the Sun. As energy is spent on its way to the top, fewer animals can be supplied with enough energy to meet their needs. Decomposers recycle food web waste from all food levels.

Top Predators
wolves, eagles, other raptors

Secondary Consumers (Carnivores and Omnivores)
scorpions, snakes, lizards, foxes

Primary Consumers (Herbivores)
grasshoppers, other insects, rodents, jackrabbits

Primary Producers (Plants)

Decomposers
beetles, fungi, bacteria

CHEW ON THIS

Ecosystems support only a few top predators, because of the large numbers of prey these hunters need to meet their energy needs. Desert food chains are short for efficiency.

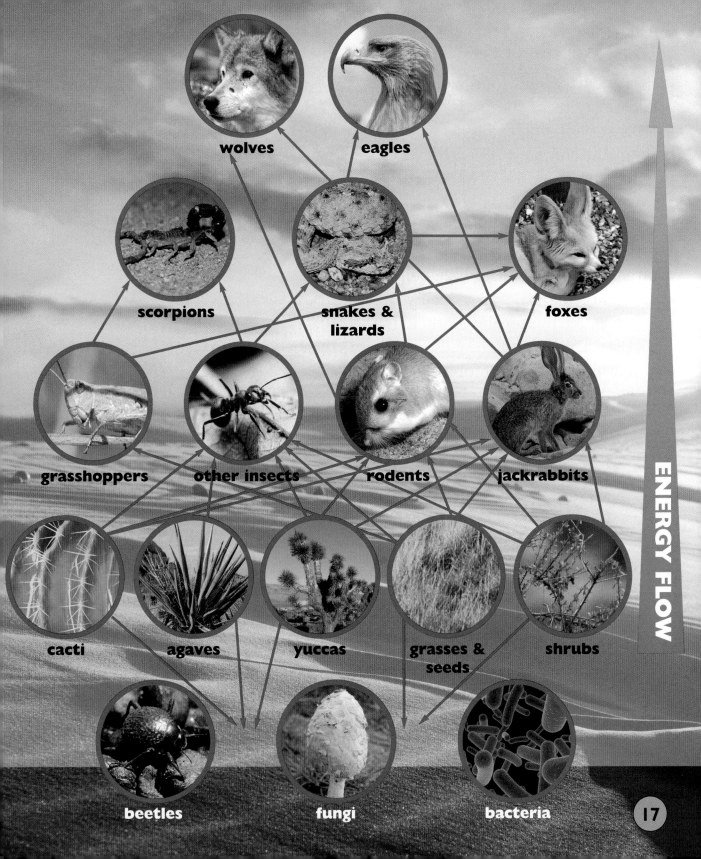

wolves

eagles

scorpions

snakes & lizards

foxes

grasshoppers

other insects

rodents

jackrabbits

ENERGY FLOW

cacti

agaves

yuccas

grasses & seeds

shrubs

beetles

fungi

bacteria

Food Web Science

To learn about food webs, ecologists trek, climb, or dig to observe living things in their environment. Because animals can be tricky to find, researchers often explore other ways of learning about an animal's diet. By examining an animal's scat for undigested animal or plant parts, ecologists can identify foods in its diet. Burrowing animals sometimes save food for later in **caches**. A careful scientist can find and inventory these caches.

CHEW ON THIS

Ecologists are scientists who study ecosystems.

The kangaroo rat packs its cheeks with seeds, and then digs shallow holes in which to store them for a later meal. A forgetful kangaroo rat helps plants by burying their seeds and leaving them behind to grow into new plants.

Ecologists investigate the diet and habits of each kind of animal to learn its role in the ecosystem. Using live traps gives researchers a quick look at *who* is in an area and *how many*. Field workers trick animals into entering the traps. They bait the traps with tasty food and camouflage them. The workers identify, measure, and weigh captured animals. They tag or mark them before release so they'll know if they catch them again. Through this sampling, ecologists snap a picture of the ecosystem.

Breaking It Down

When plants and animals die, the energy stored in their bodies isn't lost. **Scavengers** such as vultures, ravens, and coyotes help themselves to a free meal of carrion. Carrion is the bodies of dead animals. Afterwards, **decomposers** quietly dine. These include millipedes, insects, and helpful microorganisms like fungi, mold, and bacteria. They clean up the leftovers and perform a valuable service. Decomposers return necessary nutrients to the soil to be taken up by growing plants once again. It's nature's way of recycling!

CHEW ON THIS

Essential to life on Earth, tiny bacteria aid decomposition. Microorganisms work quickest when it's warm and damp. That means things decompose slowly in deserts, where the air is dry.

Many human foods would not be possible without help from microorganisms. Yeast give off gas to make bread dough rise. Bacteria thicken milk to make yogurt. Cheese makers seed their creamy blue cheese with a special fungus for that dis-STINK-tive flavor. Friendly algae stabilize the texture of ice cream.

Turkey vultures feed only on carrion. Their featherless heads and wide nostrils make it easier to clean up after gorging on rotten meat.

This Joshua tree in the Mojave Desert supports life in its shade and branches and feeds bats, birds, and rodents. If it died, 100 or more years would pass before another like it would grow.

Upsetting the Balance

Ecosystems work when everything is balanced. Removing or changing one member of a food web puts all the organisms that depend on it at risk. Delicate desert ecosystems contain life that occurs only under certain conditions, making them easily harmed. Unfortunately deserts today face many threats.

As their numbers increase, people compete with desert life for the same limited resources. Cities pump underground water up to the surface for people's daily use. As cities grow, builders bulldoze deserts for housing. In more remote areas, native predators hunt domestic animals like goats and sheep, and in turn are hunted by the herders.

Recreational vehicles compact fragile soils, cause erosion, and disturb animal burrows.

Developers clear desert land for farming or houses.

DESERT INVADERS!

In deserts, water and food are limited. When a new plant or animal arrives, it competes with native plants and animals for local resources. Aggressive invaders replace native species.

In the 1850s Europeans who had moved to Australia imported a few rabbits for hunting. The rabbits multiplied so rapidly that today millions of rabbits ravage farmers' crops and native plants alike. They burrow in huge networks of tunnels that replace the burrows of native animals and cause **erosion**. The loss of precious topsoil takes years to rebuild. Attempts at rabbit control have been disappointing and expensive.

Some U.S. ranchers planted buffelgrass, originally from Africa and Asia, for grazing cattle. Buffelgrass escaped the pastures and moved into wild desert nearby. Historically, wide spaces between desert plants prevented widespread fire. After the invasion, flammable grass filled those empty areas. Buffelgrass reseeds itself after a fire, while native plants do not.

Global Warming

Global warming is worldwide climate change. Burning fossil fuels like coal, oil, and natural gas releases carbon dioxide, a greenhouse gas. Greenhouse gases act like the glass walls of a greenhouse, trapping the Sun's heat in Earth's atmosphere. People produce greenhouse gases when they drive their cars, produce electricity, and heat their homes. As nature's air fresheners, plants naturally take in carbon dioxide and give off oxygen, but they cannot keep pace with the industrial world.

CHEW ON THIS

Sonoran Desert scientists have noticed that when temperatures rise there, they see seasonal winds, El Niño and La Niña, more often. El Niño brings more frequent rains while La Niña brings dry spells. A different climate, one that alternates wet periods with dry, could result. Climate change could shift the Sonoran Desert's ecosystem.

Global warming can increase water **evaporation** and drought. With less rainfall and more heat, young plants wither and die. Their immature root systems can't handle the lack of water. Flowers stop seed production. Without food to eat, animals must move on or die. Without vegetation to anchor them, sand dunes begin to shift and spread.

Desert Survival

To help deserts, people can learn more about them by reading, asking questions, and visiting them. Appreciating this fascinating ecosystem is the first step in stewardship, or caretaking. People can combat global warming by using energy resources wisely. Small actions like recycling, carpooling or taking a bus to school or work, and remembering to turn off lights when leaving a room help in big ways.

CHEW ON THIS

Many recycling centers accept used motor oil, clothing, cereal boxes, cardboard, phone books, and magazines in addition to paper, glass, and cans. Recycling saves energy and reduces waste in landfills.

Water conservation has importance, too. Simple ways to save water include shortening showers, repairing dripping faucets, and landscaping with native plants. By reducing the human impact on Earth, people's needs become more balanced with the needs of Earth's plants and animals.

Dramatic and in tune with the environment, native plantings promote harmony between people and desert life.

Glossary

adaptations (ad-ap-TAY-shunz): ways of survival that animals and plants have to be successful in their environment

caches (KASH-ehz): hiding places in which to store collections of things

decomposers (dee-cum-POH-zerz): animals and plants that cause rot and decay, enriching the soil with valuable nutrients

ecosystem (EE-koh-sis-tum): the relationships between all the plants and animals and the place in which they live

erosion (ee-ROH-zhun): the loss of topsoil and with it, the essential nutrients for growing plants

evaporation (ee-vap-ohr-AY-shun): the change from a liquid to a vapor, or gas

food chain (FOOD CHAYN): a series of plants and animals, each of which is eaten by the one after it

food web (FOOD WEHB): in an ecosystem, the intricate network of food chains

native (NAY-tiv): naturally occurring, living in the place where it originated

omnivores (AHM-nuh-vorz): animals that feed on a wide variety of foods including both plants and animals

photosynthesis (foh-toh-SIN-thuh-siss): the process by which green plants transform the Sun's energy into food

primary consumers (PRYE-mair-ee kahn-SOO-merz): herbivores, the animals that eat primary producers

primary producers (PRYE-mair-ee proh-DOO-serz): plants that perform photosynthesis

scavengers (SKAV-ehn-jerz): animals that eat carrion as part or all of their diet

secondary consumers (SEHK-uhn-dair-ee kuhn-SOO-merz): animals that eat herbivores

succulents (SUHK-yoo-lehnts): plants that can store large amounts of water

Further Reading

Hungry for more? Your local library serves up additional information about desert ecology and food webs. Whet your appetite with these books and websites.

Books

Aleshire, Peter. *Ten of the Most Unusual Deserts*. Chelsea House, 2008.

Fleisher, Paul. *Desert Food Webs*. Lerner, 2007.

Brezina, Corona. *Climate Change (In the News)*. Rosen, 2007.

Websites

Desert USA—The Desert Food Chain
www.desertusa.com/food_chain_k12/kids_1.html

Arizona-Sonora Desert Museum
www.desertmuseum.org/

The Flying Turtle: Exploring Science and Technology Education
www.ftexploring.com/index.html

Index

About The Author

Julie K. Lundgren grew up near Lake Superior where she reveled in mucking about in the woods, picking berries, and expanding her rock collection. Her appetite for learning about the intricate details of nature led her to a degree in biology from the University of Minnesota. She currently lives in Minnesota with her husband and two sons.

ML

WITHDRAWN